I0435149

LIBYA AT A CROSSROADS: A FALTERING TRANSITION

HEARING

BEFORE THE

SUBCOMMITTEE ON
THE MIDDLE EAST AND NORTH AFRICA

OF THE

COMMITTEE ON FOREIGN AFFAIRS
HOUSE OF REPRESENTATIVES

ONE HUNDRED THIRTEENTH CONGRESS

SECOND SESSION

JUNE 25, 2014

Serial No. 113–206

Printed for the use of the Committee on Foreign Affairs

Available via the World Wide Web: http://www.foreignaffairs.house.gov/ or http://www.gpo.gov/fdsys/

U.S. GOVERNMENT PRINTING OFFICE

88–458PDF   WASHINGTON : 2014

For sale by the Superintendent of Documents, U.S. Government Printing Office
Internet: bookstore.gpo.gov   Phone: toll free (866) 512–1800; DC area (202) 512–1800
Fax: (202) 512–2104   Mail: Stop IDCC, Washington, DC 20402–0001

COMMITTEE ON FOREIGN AFFAIRS

EDWARD R. ROYCE, California, *Chairman*

CHRISTOPHER H. SMITH, New Jersey
ILEANA ROS-LEHTINEN, Florida
DANA ROHRABACHER, California
STEVE CHABOT, Ohio
JOE WILSON, South Carolina
MICHAEL T. McCAUL, Texas
TED POE, Texas
MATT SALMON, Arizona
TOM MARINO, Pennsylvania
JEFF DUNCAN, South Carolina
ADAM KINZINGER, Illinois
MO BROOKS, Alabama
TOM COTTON, Arkansas
PAUL COOK, California
GEORGE HOLDING, North Carolina
RANDY K. WEBER SR., Texas
SCOTT PERRY, Pennsylvania
STEVE STOCKMAN, Texas
RON DeSANTIS, Florida
DOUG COLLINS, Georgia
MARK MEADOWS, North Carolina
TED S. YOHO, Florida
SEAN DUFFY, Wisconsin

ELIOT L. ENGEL, New York
ENI F.H. FALEOMAVAEGA, American Samoa
BRAD SHERMAN, California
GREGORY W. MEEKS, New York
ALBIO SIRES, New Jersey
GERALD E. CONNOLLY, Virginia
THEODORE E. DEUTCH, Florida
BRIAN HIGGINS, New York
KAREN BASS, California
WILLIAM KEATING, Massachusetts
DAVID CICILLINE, Rhode Island
ALAN GRAYSON, Florida
JUAN VARGAS, California
BRADLEY S. SCHNEIDER, Illinois
JOSEPH P. KENNEDY III, Massachusetts
AMI BERA, California
ALAN S. LOWENTHAL, California
GRACE MENG, New York
LOIS FRANKEL, Florida
TULSI GABBARD, Hawaii
JOAQUIN CASTRO, Texas

AMY PORTER, *Chief of Staff*   THOMAS SHEEHY, *Staff Director*

JASON STEINBAUM, *Democratic Staff Director*

————

SUBCOMMITTEE ON THE MIDDLE EAST AND NORTH AFRICA

ILEANA ROS-LEHTINEN, Florida, *Chairman*

STEVE CHABOT, Ohio
JOE WILSON, South Carolina
ADAM KINZINGER, Illinois
TOM COTTON, Arkansas
RANDY K. WEBER SR., Texas
RON DeSANTIS, Florida
DOUG COLLINS, Georgia
MARK MEADOWS, North Carolina
TED S. YOHO, Florida
SEAN DUFFY, Wisconsin

THEODORE E. DEUTCH, Florida
GERALD E. CONNOLLY, Virginia
BRIAN HIGGINS, New York
DAVID CICILLINE, Rhode Island
ALAN GRAYSON, Florida
JUAN VARGAS, California
BRADLEY S. SCHNEIDER, Illinois
JOSEPH P. KENNEDY III, Massachusetts
GRACE MENG, New York
LOIS FRANKEL, Florida

CONTENTS

Page

WITNESSES

The Honorable Anne W. Patterson, Assistant Secretary, Bureau of Near East-
ern Affairs, U.S. Department of State 7
The Honorable Derek Chollet, Assistant Secretary of Defense for Inter-
national Security Affairs, U.S. Department of Defense 18

LETTERS, STATEMENTS, ETC., SUBMITTED FOR THE HEARING

The Honorable Anne W. Patterson: Prepared statement 10
The Honorable Derek Chollet: Prepared statement 20

APPENDIX

Hearing notice 40
Hearing minutes 41
The Honorable Edward R. Royce, a Representative in Congress from the
State of California, and chairman, Committee on Foreign Affairs: Statement
by A Omar Turbi 42

LIBYA AT A CROSSROADS: A FALTERING TRANSITION

WEDNESDAY, JUNE 25, 2014

House of Representatives,
Subcommittee on the Middle East and North Africa,
Committee on Foreign Affairs,
Washington, DC.

The committee met, pursuant to notice, at 2 o'clock p.m., in room 2172 Rayburn House Office Building, Hon. Ileana Ros-Lehtinen (chairman of the subcommittee) presiding.

Ms. Ros-Lehtinen. The subcommittee will come to order. After recognizing myself and Ranking Member Deutch for 5 minutes each for our opening statements, I will then recognize our distinguished chairman, Mr. Royce, for as much time as he may consume. Thank you, Mr. Royce, for being with us. I will then recognize other members seeking recognition for 1 minute. We will then hear from our witnesses and without objection, the witnesses' prepared statements will be made a part of the record. Members may have 5 days to insert statements and questions for the record, subject to the length limitation in the rules. The chair recognizes herself for 5 minutes.

The Arab Spring uprising in the Middle East and North Africa of 2011 brought with them a period of brief hope for the future of democracy in the region. Millions across many nations demanded changes to the way their countries were being run and in many cases run by dictators who held a stranglehold on power for decades, unrelenting and unyielding. In some countries, the people managed to usher out the ruling party and for a moment, it appeared as though we were ready to see democracy rule the day. However, the lack of infrastructure, the lack of democratic institutions in these countries, as well the lack of political will have all but dashed those hopes and Libya, unfortunately, is one of the prime examples of this. Once Gaddafi was removed from power, those seeking to reform the government quickly proved that they were not up to the task and the country fell into a further state of disunity as armed militias battled for supremacy and control over Libya's future.

Libya has been plagued by instability, both political and economic, and its factious nature has left it on the verge of a civil war that poses very real and serious and imminent national security challenges for us in the United States. To make matters worse, the porous nature of its borders has allowed extremists to flock to Libya, adding an even greater complexity to the downward spiral and increasing the likelihood of an all out civil war. Libya has become a terrorist safe haven and the worst case scenario for all who had hoped that the Arab Spring would bring democracy to the region. We are now witnessing this crisis in Iraq and we certainly cannot afford for both nations to become entrenched safe havens for extremists to destabilize the region and attack our allies and our national security interests.

With the prevalence of so many weapons readily available to all, foreign fighters are flocking to Libya by the droves and we are seeing Libyan weapons showing up in conflicts across the entire region. So what must the United States do to help Libya avert a possible civil war, bring the political factions together to help resolve their differences, stabilize the security situation in the country, fight back the influx of extremists and shore up its borders and secure U.S. national security interests?

The problem in Libya is that there are multiple crises going on at the same time, all with their sets of issues, but all linked together and the fate of Libya resides in successfully navigating not one or some, but all of these issues. Libya cannot secure its borders, nor can it repel the extremist invasion. It cannot take advantage of its oil revenues and reserves and it cannot stabilize or stimulate its economy. The political factions remain deeply divided. And as such, the state building process has stalled, the government has not been able to establish a means to protect its borders and control the extremists or make the much needed economic reforms.

Today, the people of Libya are voting to choose members of a new Parliament. We hope that this is a new step forward into the path to stability, but as long as the security situation remains tenuous so, too, will the political transition stall and the economy falter. It is a seemingly unending spiral that leads to only further deterioration unless something is done immediately. The United States must remain engaged rather than continue its hands-off policy in Libya. We must find ways to work with the political parties to resolve their issues so that they can form a government that can de-escalate tensions and the fighting and finally get Libya back on the transition to democracy. After all, it was the administration that played a large role in the ouster of Gaddafi, but then left as quickly as we got there, leaving in our wake the mess for the Libyans to clean up themselves, knowing that they hadn't the organization or the ability to do so.

What we are witnessing today is in part a consequence of that. And we now face an uphill battle that the administration cannot sidestep or sit on the fence and hope things work in our favor. We must prevent Libya from turning into another Iraq and we must avoid this from becoming yet another tragic strategic defeat in the Middle East and North Africa for U.S. foreign policy.

And without objection, Mr. Deutch passed his turn for now and I am pleased to yield to the chairman of our committee, Mr. Royce. Thank you again for being here, Mr. Royce.

Mr. ROYCE. Well, thank you, chairwoman and Mr. Deutch, thank you very much and also welcome, Ambassador Anne Patterson, good to see you, and Mr. Chollet.

Last month, the President made a case for collective action, if you saw that speech. And indeed, coalitions were mobilized during the first Gulf War. More recently, coalitions helped end a war in Sierre Leone and hit al-Qaeda in Mali. We should always look to share the cost of actions which we take. But part of being a leader means holding our coalition partners accountable, making sure they fulfill the commitments they make. Unfortunately, this administration has failed in the role in Libya. It has been clear since the beginning that it was singularly focused on getting rid of Gaddafi, on ousting Colonel Gaddafi. The administration's lack of interest in leading has allowed our coalition partners to fail.

Despite the acknowledged weaknesses of the Libyan transitional government, this administration allowed NATO to head home knowing the job was not done. The United Nations didn't fare any better. The U.N. mission didn't fulfill even the modest task it was given. The EU was charged with border security, a commitment that was made, but never kept. The EU didn't send border security assistance teams into Libya until 2013 and only sent a portion of what was promised.

If the administration's policy was to let others take action, then the U.S. was to make sure others fulfilled their commitments. There is no doubt that the Libyans have done a lousy job guiding their country during the transition. And ultimately, the Libyans must take ownership of their future. But we can and we should be supportive. Assisting Libya today will require that we sit down with allies and partners to assess the needs. We must be clear with our allies about our shared goals and objectives and what is expected of each other.

We also need to be realistic about our own ability to accomplish our diplomatic objectives in such a dangerous environment. The protection of our diplomats must be a priority as we consider how to engage in Libya. We learned the hard lesson of the dangers of expeditionary diplomacy in Benghazi.

Today, terrorists are using Libya as a training ground and a base to destabilize the entire region. Weapons and people from across North Africa including Boko Haram and al-Qaeda in the Maghreb are meeting up in Libya and they are organizing in Libya. We know terrorists are actively trying to destabilize Tunisia and Egypt and Algeria. We know terrorists trained in Libya are fighting both in Syria and in Iraq. Libya is rapidly slipping into chaos. And as we have seen in Iraq, a terrorist element in control of valuable natural resources poses a serious threat to the state, to its neighbors and to the United States. Madam Chairwoman, I would ask unanimous consent if I could——

Ms. ROS-LEHTINEN. Not an objection.

Mr. ROYCE. This unanimous consent is for a statement of Mr. Omar Turbi to be included as part of the official record.

Ms. ROS-LEHTINEN. Thank you so very much, Mr. Chairman, for joining us. Without objection, we will make that a part of the record. We appreciate your time.

And now I am pleased to yield to my good friend, the ranking member of our subcommittee, Mr. Deutch.

Mr. DEUTCH. Thank you, Madam Chairman. Thanks for calling today's hearing. Assistant Secretaries Patterson and Chollet, welcome to the committee. And we are so pleased to have the opportunity discuss recent events in Libya and U.S. strategy toward Libya going forward.

Since the 2011 ouster of Muammar Gaddafi, Libya struggled to find its political footing, to put it mildly. What began as a promising transition to democracy has resulted in a series of rushed elections that has yielded a largely powerless central government.

Today, Libyans will again vote to elect a new representative body to replace the deadlocked General National Congress. But one must ask whether Libyan people are still invested in elections. Despite U.S. assistance focused on building up state institutions which have been virtually nonexistent for 40 years, Libya is struggling to create a strong central government that can provide both security and services to its people. The power vacuum left an opening for a well armed and well funded militant groups to seize control. In late 2013, the level of violence dramatically increased, resulting from the brazen abduction of the Libyan prime minister. 2014 has been marred by both political and security setbacks. The General National Congress has been unable to meet due to attacks by gunmen. The Ambassador of Jordan was kidnapped in Tripoli. Prime Minister Zeidan was ousted in a no confidence vote. A successor has yet to be named and a successor has yet to be named to acting Prime Minister Al-Theni and many important ministerial positions continue to remain unfilled.

As a result of the turmoil, militias have been emboldened. Militants have seized control of many of Libya's oil production facilities. Pauses in oil production have resulted in a reported loss of $30 billion creating a massive shortfall for this oil-based economy. In May, former exile, General Hifter and forces loyal to him, began launching attacks on militia groups in and around Benghazi. What exactly are General Hifter's intentions and despite his proclamation of wanting to restore security to Libya, many believe that his long-term goal is to seize government power. U.S. policy toward these actions has been unclear, as officials have expressed concern about his actions, but haven't condemned them. I hope Assistant Secretary Patterson, you can offer some clarity here today.

The general lawlessness and lack of state security has given rise to the notion that Libya is now a safe haven for terrorists. The implications of this cannot be ignored. North Africa's porous borders will provide easy transport of fighters and weapons. Libyan fighters radicalized in Syria or Iraq could easily return to Libya or any of its North African neighbors. Terrorist groups like Ansar al-Shari'a are recruiting from Libya's rural regions. These factions and others, many loosely affiliated with al-Qaeda, have reached nearly 250,000 strong. This political chaos and devolving security situation has many asking, quite frankly, why the U.S. continues to remain invested in Libya. I believe, as I stated, that the implications of letting Libya become a failed state or a terrorist safe haven are far too great for our national security. It is strategically positioned as a transit point between North Africa and the Middle East, and has water access to Europe.

Counterterrorism cooperation between our allies in these regions has to be a top priority, but do we even have a viable Libyan counterterrorism institution to partner with? Clearly, the deteriorating security situation poses the most immediate challenge, but the only way that the Libyan Government can stabilize the security situation long term is through strengthening institutions that will legitimize the government in the eyes of the Libyan people. Libya, unlike many of its Arab Spring neighbors, doesn't need U.S. dollars. It needs U.S. expertise.

Assistant Secretary Patterson, I look forward to hearing how we are continuing to provide assistance and operate programs that help build state institutions, strengthen rule of law and good governance. And I hope you will address whether the conditions set forth on the nearly $100 million of assistance we are providing continue to be met.

As we continue our efforts to train and build a capacity of the general purpose force, how can we ensure that these troops are committed to taking responsibility for Libya's security? We are unfortunately seeing the effects of an apathetic military in Iraq.

Assistant Secretary Chollet, I hope you will expand on the current status of our training programs, whether any progress has been made, and what kind of coordination is taking place among our European partners who are assisting these efforts. We know that the path to true democracy doesn't simply include holding some elections. The Libyan people spent 40 years under Gaddafi's brutal rule and they need to chart their own path forward. But I do believe that the United States is equipped to provide the kind of technical assistance needed to increase the capacity of the Libyan Government.

The deteriorating security situation has made it challenging for U.S. personnel to operate in Libya and the American public's view of Libya is undoubtedly and rightfully colored by the tragic events of September 12, 2012. This is precisely why we look to you both today to help all of us and help the American people understand why what happens in Libya in the coming months and years directly affects the United States. I thank you both for being here today and I yield back.

Ms. Ros-Lehtinen. Thank you very much, Mr. Deutch, for that opening statement.

Mr. Chabot, our subcommittee chairman.

Mr. Chabot. Thank you, Madam Chair. Ambassador Patterson, having chaired this committee in the last Congress, I have enjoyed working with you both in Egypt when I visited there a couple of times following the revolution and in your current capacity and you certainly have not shied away from the world's hot spots and we appreciate your service.

As disappointments go, Libya ranks pretty high on the list. I traveled there in 2012, a little less than a month before our friend Chris Stevens and three other brave Americans were murdered in Benghazi and while the security situation was tenuous at best, there did seem to be some sense of optimism among the Libyans I met with at that time. Gaddafi was dead and gone. Elections had been held and a new generation of leaders was convening to plan the future of a democratic Libya. Sadly, things have gone downhill since then.

Libya has abundant energy resources and port facilities that could jump start a domestic economy that was for so long controlled by a dictator. A safe and stable Libya could become a magnet for investment and tourism, but right now that is an area that seems to be a pipe dream.

I hope today we can have some productive discussion about how very dangerous and unstable Libya can get from here to there.

And Madam Chair, I would note that I have a judiciary hearing on the unprecedented numbers of children and young people coming across our southern border and so I will be sharing my time back and forth here.

Ms. ROS-LEHTINEN. Thank you so much, Mr. Chairman. And I know that there are many subcommittees and committees meeting at this time, so thank you so much.

Mr. Kennedy of Massachusetts is recognized.

Mr. KENNEDY. Thank you, Madam Chair, and thank you to the ranking member as well for holding this hearing and to our witnesses, thank you. Wonderful to see you both again. Appreciate your tremendous service to this country.

I am looking forward to your testimony today. It is obviously an extraordinarily important topic as you have heard from my colleagues. The one question I might add on top of this is trying to take a bit of a longer view as well. We have had a number of hearings in this committee over the course of the past 18 months or so about U.S. policy in various countries in North Africa and the Sahel. If you look at demographics, if you look at access to opportunity, if you look at the longer term and about the next decade or so you are having probably close to 100 million people coming of age trying to find work with very little access to transportation, food, security, healthcare or a job.

And so yes, as we are focused on and rightfully, the immediate impacts of trying to create a safe and secure Libya, as we are throughout much of this region, what are we doing to try to make sure we are not putting out fires here every day for the next 10, 15, 20 years?

Thank you, Madam Chair. I yield back.

Ms. ROS-LEHTINEN. Thank you, Mr. Kennedy. Mr. Weber of Texas is recognized.

Mr. WEBER. I am ready to get going.

Ms. ROS-LEHTINEN. Thank you very much, sir. Mr. Connolly of Virginia is recognized.

Mr. CONNOLLY. Thank you, Madam Chairman, and thank you for holding this hearing. I just think that in some ways this hearing is very timely and very opportune, but Libya is a bit of a morality tale about how limited our reach can be. There are lots of people who wanted us to intervene in a very robust way during the Arab Spring, but I am not sure, even had we done that, the outcomes we are looking at today would have been very different. And that is the problem. It is great to feel wonderful in the beginning of a revolution, but generally a lot of revolutions have bad outcomes or less than desirable and noble outcomes. And I think we are seeing that in Libya today.

So I am going to be very interested in hearing the testimony, but what is our part to leverage and influence the future course of Libya in a way that we hope is democratic and open and inclusive and that serves our interests as well those of Libya's?

Thank you, Madam Chairman.

Ms. Ros-Lehtinen. Thank you, Mr. Connolly. Mr. DeSantis of Florida. Dr. Yoho. Let us go. Thank you.

And now we are pleased to introduce our panelists. First, we welcome back a good friend of our subcommittee, Ambassador Anne Patterson, who is Assistant Secretary of State for Near Eastern Affairs. Ambassador Patterson has been our U.S. Ambassador to El Salvador, Colombia, Pakistan, and most recently, Egypt. She has also served as Assistant Secretary of State for International Narcotics and Law Enforcement Affairs, Deputy Permanent Representative to the United Nations and Deputy Inspector General at the State Department. Welcome, Madam Ambassador.

We also have with us Mr. Derek Chollet who is the Assistant Secretary of Defense for International Security Affairs. Prior to this position, he served in the White House as Special Assistant to the President and Senior Director for Strategic Planning on the National Security Council staff and at the State Department as the principal Deputy Director of the Secretary's Policy Planning staff. Thank you both for being here. As I said, your remarks will be made a part of the record and feel free to summarize. We will begin with you, Honorable Ambassador Patterson.

STATEMENT OF THE HONORABLE ANNE W. PATTERSON, ASSISTANT SECRETARY, BUREAU OF NEAR EASTERN AFFAIRS, U.S. DEPARTMENT OF STATE

Ambassador Patterson. Thank you, Chairman Ros-Lehtinen, Ranking Member Deutch, members of the subcommittee, for inviting me to discuss the situation in Libya and the administration's response.

Libya's transition faces significant challenges that will require intensive engagement by the U.S. and our international partners for many years. Since the fall of the Gaddafi regime, Libyans have been struggling to build a stable and effective democratic government that provides a secure environment and economic opportunity. The stakes for the United States, as well as for the Libyan people, are substantial.

Libya is a relatively large country with a comparatively small population whose unifying ties are relatively weak and where strong, local and tribal ties make national unity difficult. During the past 3 years, the national government has been unable to provide adequate security and services for its people. Weapons from Gaddafi's substantial caches have floated on to the market, some traveling across borders into the Sinai and into Syria.

The security vacuum has permitted over 100 militias and other armed groups dissatisfied with the government to target critical oil infrastructure, disrupt the economy, and incite tensions between Islamist and secularist groups. Judges, politicians, and civic leaders are routinely murdered. Working with our colleagues at DoD and the FBI, militia leader, Ahmet Abu Khattala, was removed from the battlefield and will face U.S. justice.

Amidst this chaos, Libya's oil production, the sole source of government revenue, has fallen to 20 percent of capacity around 280,000 barrels per day. These disruptions have severely hampered Libya's economy and ripple through the entire country, amounting to up to $30 billion in lost revenue.

U.S. national security interests require vigorous U.S. engagement to support Libya. We are pursuing several important initiatives to try and arrest further political and security instability and to help revive Libya's private sector so it can play a crucial role in stabilizing the country and we would like to do more.

First, in the immediate term, we are urging Libyans to agree to general principles to build consensus and guide the remainder of the political transition and stressing that political differences must be settled through dialogue and compromise. Ambassador David Satterfield is meeting intensively and working closely with key Libyan stakeholders, U.K. special envoy Jonathan Powell, and with U.N. and international envoys.

Second, we are working with Libya, its neighbors, and the international community to strengthen Libya's internal security and tightening border security.

Finally, once there is sufficient political stability and security, we have created a framework that partner countries will use to coordinate their assistance in key areas. We are also encouraging the U.S. private sector to come in and help rebuild Libya's economy and its institutions.

Despite the many worrying events, we do see some positive steps occurring in Libya's economy and in its democratic transition. Last week, I spoke at a symposium at the Wilson Center that focused on rebuilding Libya's economy. The experts and Libyan ex-patriots acknowledged the many challenges Libya poses for companies interested in investing there. But they also underscore Libya's great economic potential and how Libyans generally want U.S. companies to invest there.

We are currently providing more than $100 million in assistance to Libya. Given the government's historic weaknesses, one of our crucial missions is to train Libyans in the fundamentals of public administration and finance. We have also focused our efforts together with our European partners on promoting democratic processes that are crucial for long-term stability and we have been providing targeted technical security assistance such as securing and neutralizing Gaddafi era chemical weapons stockpiles. Libya is now free of all weapons of mass destruction.

Today in Libya, voters went to the polls to elect a new legislature to be called the Council of Representatives. Today's elections are a milestone in Libya's transition and a symbol of Libya's continued commitment to democracy.

Libya's constitutional drafting assembly has also begun drafting a new Constitution which we are hopeful will create a new Constitution that will include separation of powers and respect for the dignity of all Libyans.

Madam Chairman, Ranking Member Deutch, we approach our diplomatic engagement with Libya with our eyes wide open. To protect our national security interests and to preserve broad future opportunities for U.S. companies, we need a sustained, diplomatic engagement with Libya. We will continue to consult with the Congress as we go forward, but we will need to broaden our support to Libya with a range of programs in the months ahead. It is my view that we will need to expand our in-country diplomatic and development presence and activities.

Thank you, Madam Chairman.
[The prepared statement of Ambassador Patterson follows:]

Statement for the Record
Ambassador Anne W. Patterson
Assistant Secretary of State for Near Eastern Affairs

House Foreign Affairs Committee
Subcommittee on the Middle East and North Africa
June 25, 2014

Thank you, Chairman Ros-Lehtinen, Ranking Member Deutch, Members of the Subcommittee, for inviting me to discuss the situation in Libya and the Administration's response.

Libya's democratic transition faces a number of significant challenges that will require intensive work by both Libyans and their international partners over a long period. Achieving and maintaining a stable democracy that provides Libyans with an effective government, a secure environment for Libyans and foreigners alike, and economic opportunity will not be easy. But the stakes for us, as well as for the Libyan people, are substantial.

Libya has the largest coastline of any country on the Mediterranean, and transportation routes and access to nearly the entire Middle East. If Libya does not develop a functioning and stable democratic government, it could transmit instability well beyond its immediate borders to threaten three vital areas: the Sahel, North Africa and the Mediterranean.

To help Libya achieve the promise heralded by its people throwing off the chains of the Qadhafi regime, we are engaged in four major ongoing areas of effort. First, as the recent arrest of Abu Khattala for his alleged role in the murder of four Americans in Benghazi highlights, we are continuing vigorous counter-terrorism efforts. Second, through our diplomacy and direct assistance, we are working to strengthen security institutions and build governance capacity. Third, we are supporting the democratic transition processes through elections, constitution drafting, and national dialogue. Fourth, we are seeking to promote economic development so that the private sector in Libya becomes a significant driver of stability. Each of these efforts faces substantial challenges.

Libya's Challenges

While Libya does not face the daunting sectarian strife that plagues some Arab countries in transition, it lacks many crucial governmental capacities and must build a modern infrastructure from the ground up. Four decades of mismanagement under Qadhafi caused significant damage. Libya lacks modern governmental institutions and a professional bureaucracy capable of meeting the needs and expectations of the Libyan people.

The violence in Libya is alarming. It has spread from the East to the West, and has grown through the early months of 2014. The government has been unable to stabilize the country or stop the now-routine killings and kidnappings. The Libyan people, after bravely coming together to overthrow a brutal dictator, must now live with violence exacerbated by the presence of more than one hundred destabilizing militias that serve under no common authority and which live under no overriding system of laws or law enforcement structures.

On average over the past year, one to two people have been killed every day in eastern Libya. Judges, politicians and civic leaders have been murdered for trying to do their jobs. The security vacuum has also permitted militias and other groups dissatisfied with the central government to target critical oil infrastructure and to negatively influence political developments. As a result, Libya's oil production – the sole source of government revenue – has fallen to as low as 10 percent of capacity or about 150,000 barrels per day. These disruptions have severely hampered Libya's economy and rippled through the entire country, amounting to up to $30 billion in lost revenues that could have gone to financing the transition.

Political Steps Forward

All of this has created a situation in Libya that is unstable, and which threatens to destabilize even further if its leaders fail to come together for the benefit of the Libyan people. The Libyan government has been unable to provide adequate security and services for its people; confidence in the government is low and its institutions are facing a legitimacy crisis that threatens the country's democratic transition. Deepening political divisions between Islamist and non-Islamist political elements vying for power have compounded the instability. Although some of the myriad militia groups provide policing services to communities, they have not been integrated into a national system to provide security for Libyans overall, and because they are not integrated, have different constituencies, different goals, and are not undertaking their work under a legal framework or system of oversight, their overall effect is incredibly destabilizing.

Libya's political factions need to find a path through all of this to build institutions. To facilitate that process, Secretary Kerry has asked Ambassador David Satterfield to work closely with UK Special Envoy Jonathan Powell and with key Libyan stakeholders, in coordination with the UN and international envoys. We are urging Libyans to agree to general principles to guide the remainder of the political transition and we are stressing that political differences must be settled through dialogue and compromise, not violence.

As this political dialogue progresses, we're also working with Libya, its neighbors, and the international community to strengthen Libya's internal security while mitigating the extent that instability or loose weapons that now saturate Libya can leak across its borders. As we've seen in other parts of the region, one country's instability can quickly spread over shared borders and destabilize a neighbor. We have had successful programs in isolating and separating out Libya's residual chemical weapons precursors. We are also engaged with the European Union and with neighboring countries to enhance efforts against traffickers, smugglers, and terrorists seeking to take advantage of Libya's large and historically porous borders.

Additionally, we are participating in frameworks with other countries – the Paris Ministerial matrices and the Rome Ministerial compacts – to coordinate assistance in key areas, such as good governance and enhanced security, and we are having regular discussions with the U.S. private sector on steps needed to rebuild Libya's economy and its institutions. These initiatives will help construct the foundation for further progress in Libya, but their ultimate success will depend on Libya finding mechanisms to turn national dialogue into the development of a constitution and a system of governance that is inclusive, democratic, and stable.

Today in Libya, voters went to the polls to elect a new legislature, the Council of Representatives, which will replace the General National Congress. Today's elections are a milestone in Libya's transition and Libya's continued commitment to democracy. In addition, Libya has successfully held over 70 municipal elections in the past year, promoting democratic development at the local level.

Another encouraging sign is that following national elections in February, Libya's Constitution Drafting Assembly has begun drafting a new constitution. This is a difficult process but we're hopeful that with support from the international community, the drafters will create a new constitution that will include the separation of powers and will respect the dignity of all Libyans, including minorities and women. We would like this process to lead to the creation of a strong civil state with strong institutions.

It was also very encouraging to see a political crisis defused peacefully earlier this month when the Supreme Court in Libya ruled in favor of one of two competing prime ministers – and the losing party vacated the Prime Minister's office he had inhabited only a week earlier. This demonstrates the capacity of the Libyan people and their institutions to overcome political challenges.

Assistance from the USG and International Partners

Madam Chairman, transitions to democracies are notoriously difficult endeavors, but we have an opportunity to support Libya's transition in a productive direction; moreover, the majority of Libyans want a close relationship with the United States. The opportunity to stand with this majority will not stay open forever if this majority loses faith in a peaceful and democratic transition.

Let me briefly describe our assistance efforts. The United States is currently providing more than $100 million in assistance to Libya. We have focused, together with our European partners, on promoting the basis for a democratic transition, including through support for the development of an independent press, a nascent civil society, and Libya's first free and fair elections in July 2012, as well as those underway today. We have also been providing targeted technical security assistance, such as securing and neutralizing Qadhafi-era chemical weapons stockpiles and reigning in loose conventional weapons. As of early 2014, Libya has been free of all chemical weapons.

Security remains a top priority. As a result, we're working closely with the European Union Border Assistance Mission to train and equip border security officials so that they can effectively manage and secure Libya's porous borders. And we have pledged to train several thousand General Purpose Forces, which will represent a force of well-trained recruits whose job will be to strengthen Libya's capacity to protect the Libyan people as well as ensure its territorial sovereignty. My colleague, Assistant Secretary Chollet, will speak in more detail about the General Purpose Forces.

Our security assistance is designed to help Libya control the rampant violence that has paralyzed the country, and to give the new government the breathing room it needs to regain legitimacy and chart a constructive path forward. This work is necessary to create an environment where democracy, good governance, and a healthy civil society and private sector can take root and thrive.

In his West Point address last month, President Obama emphasized that when this Administration acts overseas on behalf of human dignity and as a matter of national security, we should not expect change to happen overnight. He noted: "That's why we form alliances not just with governments, but also with ordinary people. For unlike other nations, America is not afraid of individual empowerment, we're strengthened by it. We're strengthened by civil society. We're strengthened by a free press. We're strengthened by striving entrepreneurs and small businesses. We're strengthened by educational exchanges and opportunity for all people, and women and girls."

Madam Chairman, consistent with this strategic vision we are devoting significant resources to help the Libyan government and civil society groups in their work to lay the foundations of a new democratic society. Our assistance aims to further support inclusive national reconciliation processes, consultative constitution drafting, and healthy election cycles.

While Libya is a wealthy country, it is new to democracy and continues to struggle to build effective institutions. One of our crucial missions is to help the Libyan government develop the capacity to fund and provide services to meet the expectations of its people. This means helping to stand up civil administrators who can ensure the government's bills are paid, the lights turn on and the trash gets picked up on time. This limited capacity contributes to the low confidence most Libyans have in their governing institutions and also has meant that large grants and infrastructure projects that donor countries would like to provide, projects that could alleviate hardships Libyans face day-in-and-day-out, flounder because there's no administrative capacity to carry them out.

The International Partnership for Libya, which Secretary Kerry announced at the Rome Ministerial in March, is designed to ensure that the assistance pledged at the Rome Ministerial in support of Libya's transition is successfully implemented. In an another encouraging sign of the international community's commitment, over forty international delegations participated in this meeting and echoed the Secretary's emphasis on Libya's need for stronger government institutions capable of managing budgets, programs, and personnel as well as improved security.

Conclusion

Madam Chairman, Ranking Member Deutch, I can assure you that we approach our diplomatic engagement with Libya with our eyes wide open. This will be a long-term endeavor but it is in our national security interest to do whatever we can in support of a successful Libyan transition.

Thank you.

———

18

Ms. Ros-Lehtinen. Thank you, Madam Ambassador.
Mr. Chollet.

STATEMENT OF THE HONORABLE DEREK CHOLLET, ASSISTANT SECRETARY OF DEFENSE FOR INTERNATIONAL SECURITY AFFAIRS, U.S. DEPARTMENT OF DEFENSE

Mr. Chollet. Thank you, Madam Chair, Ranking Member Deutch, members of the subcommittee. I am grateful to speak to you this afternoon about Libya and the Defense Department's approach for addressing Libya's immense security challenges. I will focus my remarks on four issues: The general purpose force, counterterrorism training, border security, and our efforts to secure the U.S. Embassy in Tripoli.

First, the key factor in Libya's transition is security and the successful development of the Libyan armed forces. Last year, at the request of the then Libyan prime minister, the United States committed to help train a Libyan General Purpose Force of 5,000 to 8,000 personnel. This kind of force will help the Libyan Government form its core military. Libya has committed to fully fund this training which is estimated at roughly $600 million over the duration of the program which can take up to 8 years. In this effort, when started, will be executed by our Africa command. And I want to stress that building Libya's military is not an American effort alone. It has strong international support from others including the United Kingdom, Italy, and Turkey which have all begun training and have committed to training a combined 7,000 personnel in the coming years. And just yesterday, 255 troops trained by Italy completed their training and returned to Libya.

So although the United States stands by this commitment, progress has been slow. Several factors have hampered the execution of our training mission. The most important is Libya's political turmoil and a deteriorating security situation which makes it difficult to have the necessary U.S. personnel on the ground in Tripoli to execute this program. Other factors include a lack of vetted training candidates, a lack of pledged Libyan funding, and weak security institutions.

To help build Libya's security institutions and enhance military professionalism, the Defense Department recently had 40 Libyan military personnel attending U.S. professional education courses, including senior service colleges via the IMET program. And additionally, the Libyans have funded a national security seminar for 25 Libyan military leaders to be students at NDU, National Defense University, last year. We also hope to provide defense advisors to the Libyan Ministry of Defense in the future via the Ministry of Defense Advisor Programs and the Defense Institution Reform Initiative.

Now in addition to this effort to build a general purpose for us, the second line of effort is working with the Libyan Government to develop its counterterrorism capacity through the Global Security Contingency Fund. And this will help train several hundred Libyan special forces personnel.

Third, as was mentioned, Libya's border regions have become major areas of instability and the cross border movement of violent extremists, the trafficking of weapons and the massive influx of immigrants is deeply concerning. This is especially a worry to those countries such as Egypt and Italy, who are the recipients of the flow of Libya's weapons and people. And with congressional support we have developed a program to help build Libya's border security capacity through the Global Security Contingency Fund. And we are coordinating our efforts with the European Union who has focused its program on border security.

And fourth, on Embassy security, we maintain a laser focus on the immense challenges and risks of operating in an uncertain security environment and we will do what it takes to protect our people and to bring to justice those who do us harm. Given our concerns about security in Tripoli, we have placed additional U.S. military forces in the region to respond to a variety of contingencies and stand ready to respond as needed. Alongside our efforts to prevent attacks, we also maintain an unrelenting commitment to hold accountable to those who harm Americans.

And Madam Chair, as this committee knows, and as Ambassador Patterson mentioned, on June 15th the U.S. captured Abu Khatallah who was a key figure in the September 11, 2012 attacks in Benghazi. The success of this mission was due to the combined efforts of our military, law enforcement, and intelligence personnel, and as the President stressed just last week, with this operation, the United States has once again demonstrated that we will do whatever it takes to see that justice is done when people harm Americans.

Madam Chair, Ranking Member Deutch, and members of the subcommittee, after the fall of Gaddafi in the fall of 2011, President Obama made clear that ''we are under no illusions. Libya will travel a long and winding road to full democracy and there will be difficult days ahead. And we have been living through those days recently. But the United States, together with the international community, is committed to the Libyan people.'' And so with this in mind, we continue to support Libya's transition and to do so we will work closely with the Libyans, our international partners, and the Congress. Although our efforts have been complicated by Libya's tumultuous politics and tense security environment, we remain committed to strengthening Libya's security institutions.

Thank you, and I look forward to your questions.

[The prepared statement of Mr. Chollet follows:]

Assistant Secretary of Defense Derek Chollet
International Security Affairs
U.S. Department of Defense

House Foreign Affairs Middle East and North Africa Subcommittee
"Security Situation in Libya"
June 25, 2014; 2:00pm to 4:00pm

Madam Chairman Ros-Lehtinen, Ranking Member Deutch, and Members of the

Subcommittee, I appreciate the opportunity to speak to you today about the security situation in

Libya and the Defense Department's approach for addressing these challenges.

Introduction

Libya remains a country in transition, and the path towards stability continues to present

a series of challenges. Libya's institutions across the board remain weak, and the Ministry of

Defense is no exception. Qaddafi's style of rule and his reliance on non-Libyan paramilitary

forces to guard his regime at the expense of the armed forces left little in the way of functioning

national institutions after his removal. The United States and its many partners have since

grappled with the immense difficulties of helping Libya rebuild its political and security

institutions. The effect of Qaddafi's legacy, particularly his deep neglect of the Libyan Armed

Forces, has left the current government unable to provide security for its own institutions or

critical infrastructure, disarm militias, or exercise control over the country's vast borders. As a

result, the Libyan government's reach and capacity is severely limited, and it is forced to rely on

unruly militias to provide a semblance of security and rule of law. Moreover, violent extremist

groups have exploited Libya's permissive security environment to establish a presence in the

country and to smuggle fighters and weapons across its borders, helping to fuel instability across

the region and stirring alarm among Libya's neighbors in North Africa, Europe, and the Sahel.

The Department of Defense is prioritizing its assistance to focus on building Libya's security capacity and improving the government's ability to counter terrorism, protect government institutions and key infrastructure, and counter weapons proliferation. Since 2011, we have sought to build a partnership with Libya based on shared interests and our strong support for Libya's democratic transition. I will use my opening remarks to touch on our work with the Libyan General Purpose Force, CT training programs, border security initiatives, the elimination of chemical weapons, and embassy security efforts.

General Purpose Force

First, I would like to address our efforts to strengthen the defense capabilities of the Libyan government. The Department of Defense recognizes that a key element of Libya's transition is the successful development of the Libyan Armed Forces. Now more than ever, Libya needs capable armed forces under the control of a democratically elected central government.

At the request of the Libyan government, last year the United States committed to train a General Purpose Force (GPF) of 5,000-8,000 Libyan military personnel. This training effort is intended to help the government form the core of the military it requires to protect government institutions and key infrastructure, and to maintain law and order. The Government of Libya has committed to fund this training program fully through a Foreign Military Sales case, and has provided initial funding. We anticipate that the U.S.-led GPF training program will begin at a joint U.S.-Bulgarian training facility in Bulgaria later this year and continue for five to eight years.

As with the 2011 effort to protect the Libyan people from the brutality of the Qaddafi regime, the effort to help build Libya's security forces has strong international support. We are joined by partners who share our interest in supporting the Libyan government as it works to bring stability to the country. The United Kingdom, Italy, and Turkey are also taking part in the GPF training effort and have committed to training a total of 7,000 additional Libyan personnel. We are working in close coordination with these countries and Libya and have successfully standardized the training programs among all GPF training providers. Although we and our partners' programs are at different stages of planning and execution, the output of trained Libyan military personnel is intended to be very similar. The Turkish, Italian, and U.K. training programs have already begun and we continue to assess their lessons learned as we move forward.

Several factors have hampered the execution of our GPF training program. The GPF concept was initially conceived last spring by then-Libyan Prime Minister Ali Zeidan. Zeidan's abrupt departure from office in March 2014 and the ensuing political turmoil and turnover in senior political and military leaders have disrupted our progress. The deteriorating security environment in Tripoli has also proven difficult, and the security vacuum in the capital inhibits the ability of Defense Department personnel to operate on the ground. Despite these setbacks, we continue to work with Libyan officials when possible to ensure all training candidates are properly prepared for training, meet human rights standards in accordance with U.S. law, and have no known associations with extremist groups. At this stage, two important steps remain for U.S. GPF training to commence, specifically Libyan approval of the Letter of Offer and Acceptance and allocation of funding in addition to the approval of the bilateral technical agreement between Libya and Bulgaria.

Madam Chairman, the GPF training program is a large part of a broader, comprehensive effort, by the United States, our European Allies, NATO, the European Union, and the United Nations to rebuild and strengthen Libya's defense institutions. This includes the provision of technical assistance and advice through bilateral efforts from our European Allies and the UN Support Mission in Libya. Additionally, NATO has agreed in principle to a Libyan request to provide an advisory team to the Libyan Ministry of Defense, but has not yet received Libyan approvals. The United States is acting in close coordination with our partner nations and international organizations to provide effective support to Libya's defense institutions.

CT Training Programs

Second, the Department of Defense is working with the Libyan government to develop its capacity to conduct counterterrorism operations. With congressional support, we have funded programs to develop Libya's counter-terrorism forces via a joint State-DoD Global Security Contingency Fund (GSCF) program to train two companies of Libyan Special Operations Forces ($7.75M) and a program to train and equip a Libyan Special Operations Forces support company ($8.42M) using the "global train and equip" authority of Section 1206 of the National Defense Authorization Actor for Fiscal Year 2006, as amended. We believe that these programs will positively impact Libya's security situation. The programs should begin soon.

Border Security

Third, Libya's border regions have become a major area of instability as a result of the prolonged political unrest, escalating violence, and the limited capacity of the Libyan central government. The cross-border movement of violent extremists, the trafficking of weapons and other illicit goods, and the massive influx of migrants using Libyan ports as a point of departure are also causing alarm among Libya's neighbors and our European allies. France, Algeria, and Tunisia have expressed serious concerns about Libya's western and southwestern border areas, specifically regarding the flow of extremists and weapons between Libya, Mali, and the Sahel region. Egypt is also troubled by the deteriorating security situation in Eastern Libya. Earlier this month, Egypt announced that it would close its main northwestern border crossing with Libya following a series of clashes between its border guards and heavily armed smugglers. Libya's expansive maritime borders are also proving to be a source of instability. Since October 2013, Italy has conducted an extensive maritime security and rescue operation in the Mediterranean Sea in response to an unprecedented wave of migration. Italian officials have reported that more than 50,000 migrants have arrived in their country in 2014—many coming by way of Libyan ports.

The situation along Libya's borders is concerning to the United States and our partners. To help address these problems, we are pursuing a $14.9M program under GSCF authority to build Libya's inter-ministerial border security capacity. This program is still in the planning stages as we have had to re-scope our initial plans due in large part to our inability to travel freely in Libya. We are coordinating our efforts with the European Union Border Assistance Mission to train and equip Libyan border security officials.

Chemical Weapons

Fourth, while the United States has been working on long-term efforts to strengthen Libya's security institutions since the fall of the Qaddafi regime, we have also assisted Libya with the destruction of its remaining weapons of mass destruction. I am pleased to report to the

Committee that Libya is free of weapons of mass destruction since January 2014. Furthermore, there is no evidence that any chemical weapons or agents remain in Libya.

The destruction of Libya's chemical weapons stockpile was achieved through the Department of Defense's Cooperative Threat Reduction (CTR) Program, which complemented efforts by the Department of State's Nonproliferation and Disarmament Fund. The Defense Threat Reduction Agency implemented this effort using contractors for all on-the-ground work. The total cost of the program reached approximately $50M. The destruction was realized through close cooperation between the U.S. and Libyan governments and international partners— especially Germany and Canada—and was overseen by the Organisation for the Prohibition of Chemical Weapons (OPCW). This accomplishment demonstrates that even war-torn nations can declare and eliminate their chemical agents and weapons in a safe and timely fashion.

Embassy Security

Lastly, I would like to address U.S. Embassy security, and the recent capture of Ahmed Abu Khatallah. While we work to foster a partnership with Libya, we continue to be mindful of the immense challenges and risks operating in an uncertain security environment. We are very concerned about the rising violence and continued political instability in Libya and we continue to monitor developments there closely. The Defense Department is committed to the protection of U.S. personnel and facilities around the world and is prepared to respond to a variety of situations. On several occasions, the Department of Defense, in close coordination and consultation with the State Department, has forward-positioned and changed the readiness status of crisis response forces in the region in response to heightened threats.

Due to the recent political unrest and renewed fighting in Tripoli and Benghazi, the Department of Defense forward-positioned additional U.S. military forces to support our diplomatic presence in Libya. The Department of Defense stands ready to respond to a crisis and take action to protect U.S. personnel and facilities in Libya.

Abu Khatallah Capture

Madam Chairman, as you are aware, on June 15, the U.S. military, in cooperation with U.S law enforcement personnel, conducted a successful operation in Libya in which Abu Khatallah was captured. Abu Khatallah is a key figure in the September 11, 2012, attacks on U.S. facilities in Benghazi in which Ambassador Christopher Stevens and three other Americans were killed. Until his capture, Khatallah was a senior leader of the militant group Ansar al-Sharia in Benghazi, which is designated by the Department of State as a Foreign Terrorist Organization. There were no civilian casualties in this operation, and all U.S. personnel involved are safe. Abu Khatallah is in U.S. custody in a secure location outside Libya. The success of this mission was due to the extraordinary capabilities and efforts of our military, law enforcement, and intelligence personnel, and our unrelenting commitment to hold accountable those who harm Americans.

Conclusion

Madam Chairman Ros-Lehtinen, Ranking Member Deutch, and Members of the Subcommittee, amid the hope for Libya's future after the fall of the Qaddafi regime in October 2011, President Obama said, "We're under no illusions — Libya will travel a long and winding road to full democracy. There will be difficult days ahead. But the United States, together with the international community, is committed to the Libyan people. You have won your revolution. And now, we will be a partner as you forge a future that provides dignity, freedom and opportunity." We continue to support Libya's transition, which includes parliamentary elections underway today, and work closely with the Libyans and international partners toward that end. The Defense Department will prudently continue to address the challenges and risks in Libya and will be clear-sighted about what we can accomplish and how quickly. Although helping Libya during this period of instability is a difficult task, it is important to stress that Libya's democratically elected leaders have been willing and eager partners in terms of strengthening military ties with the United States and our allies and partners. Although at times our engagements have been complicated by Libyan politics and the security environment, our commitment to strengthen Libya's security institutions during its democratic transition has not wavered.

I look forward to your questions.

———————

Ms. Ros-Lehtinen. Thank you very much to both of our witnesses and I will begin with the question and answer period. Thank you.

Libya is as unstable as ever and the current government, as you testified, Mr. Chollet, is unable to provide security for its own institutions, infrastructure, or exercise control over its vast and porous borders. Our efforts to strengthen the defense capabilities of the Libyan Government is this General Purpose Force, but we haven't even begun training them 3 years after Gaddafi. So what were we doing these past 3 years while Libya became the wild, wild West? Why didn't we remain engaged, knowing that the Libyan people would be ill equipped, ill prepared to face the immediate challenges and how has our disengagement contributed to the current situation on the ground?

We know that Gaddafi had a large stockpile of weapons and even sealed stockpiles of chemical weapons and that once he fell, it was a mad dash to try to recover those. We even allocated over $40 million in an effort to keep them out of terrorist hands, yet Libyan arms have been used not only in Libya, but in Mali, in Algeria, Tunisia, Chad, Lebanon, and Syria, probably everywhere else.

Furthermore, Qatar was shipping weapons to Libyan rebels despite an arms embargo on Libya during the 2011 uprisings and we did nothing to stop that. In fact, many sources say we condoned it. Unsurprisingly, many of these weapons fell into the hands of terrorists. How did we fail to recover Gaddafi's arms and actually end up indirectly supplying the terrorists with even more weapons? And what is the status of our efforts on that front now? How heavily armed are these groups today?

Ambassador Patterson, today, the people of Libya are going to the polls, as we have said, to select members of their new Parliament. However, it seems that the administration is bent on keeping its hands off policy in Libya despite seeing where that has gotten us. Reuters published an article last night about our policy in today's election and it quotes an unnamed U.S. Government official saying that our policy won't change significantly no matter what the outcome of the elections are and the administration has acknowledged there is only so much that it can do in Libya. Is that our Libya policy? We help create the mess, but we are going to keep as far away as possible that we can't do anything to right the ship?

And the rapidly deteriorating security situation certainly looms heavy over this election. The timing of the election was also rushed as they were only announced last month. What has the administration done to help the Libyans ensure that the elections are credible and that the results will be truly representative of the people of Libya? Can you give us the latest assessment on the elections? What are the major issues? How do we plan to deal with the new government to reverse course in Libya? Thank you to both.

Mr. Chollet?

Mr. Chollet. Thanks, Madam Chair. On the issue of Libyan weapons, for many years it has been a great concern of ours. The amount of weapons in Libya and the flow of those weapons outside of Libya, whether it is headed toward Mali or across into Egypt. We have had some successes, particularly, for example, on the chemical weapons issue which was a very concerning situation after the fall of Gaddafi and through our efforts we helped secure the chemical weapons facility in Wadan, but then very importantly over the course of 2013 spent about $50 million to help destroy weaponized munitions that had been undeclared prior to the fall of Gaddafi, so identify those, secure those munitions and then ultimately destroy them. That was administered through our Cooperative Threat Reduction Program.

Secondly, on MANPADS, shoulder fired air defense missiles, again, Libya had a tremendously large stockpile of these weapons that Gaddafi had amassed. And the Department of Defense, working very closely with our partners in Department of State, spent roughly $40 million to help identify and destroy large stocks of those MANPADS. So we feel as though even though we are still very concerned, there are some successes we have had.

Very quickly on the General Purpose Force and the training effort, as I said in my statement we are not where we want to be on that effort. There are many reasons for that. It is only a year ago that the Libyans asked for assistance in training such a force, so we have worked very hard, the Department of Defense through my office, through AFRICOM, but with our State Department colleagues as well on scaling up this effort. One of the reasons why it has been slow is because our Libyan partners and the lack of capacity on their end to help hold up their end of the bargain in terms of paying for this program. As I mentioned, it is about $600 million, at least our piece of it, to be scoped.

It is important to note that our allies with the gun training, modestly, are doing so out of pocket. The Libyans have not paid them so the training that they are doing is something they are doing out of their own budgets. But the second issue, I would just say the problem of identifying and vetting Libyan personnel. We want to make sure that the folks that we do train are qualified and capable of being trained and one of the challenges we face is given the security environment we can't have the personnel on the ground in Tripoli right now to help execute this program. So there is a chicken and an egg situation here where security is a huge problem, but because of the lack of security, we can't have the necessary personnel on the ground to help execute programs to improve Libyan security. So that is the dilemma we face.

Ms. ROS-LEHTINEN. Thank you, sir. Ambassador Patterson?

Ambassador PATTERSON. Madam Chairman, I heard this morning that 97 percent of the polls opened on time. Participation seems steady, but slow, but it is 112 degrees there, so they are hoping that participation will go up in the afternoon. I think, Madam Chairman, that we have tried to be very much engaged in this electoral process. We trained over 400 election observers. We provided three advisors to the Electoral Commission through IFA, a very respected institution. National Democratic Institute is working with political parties to train particularly young people and women, and to do capacity training. And then we have funded civil society organizations who are promoting voting mobilization and voter education. So we have tried and I can talk about the Constitution process, too. So we have tried to totally lean forward and support this election process which is going okay so far and we are hoping that it will result in a new legislature in a few weeks.

Madam Chairman, we have a program should the political situation and security situation stabilize, to very substantially increase our presence and our involvement in Libya because the range of what they need, as Mr. Deutch noticed, is technical assistance more than money. They have a crying need for assistance on issues like public finance and budget management or managing the revenues from the petroleum sector. And we are very anxious to be engaged with them in those areas. So we are planning to up our capacity there.

As Derek says, a lot of it comes down to the amount of risk we are willing to take and the amount of people we are willing to put on the ground. Thank you.

Ms. ROS-LEHTINEN. Thank you very much. And now I turn to the ranking member. Mr. Deutch, for his questions.

Mr. DEUTCH. Thank you, Madam Chairman. Assistant Secretary Patterson, why is the U.S. in Libya? What are our interests? What is our strategy for operating there if the current security situation remains unchanged?

Ambassador PATTERSON. The most urgent, if I could say, the most urgent objective we have is counterterrorism. Because it is critical that Libya not become essentially an ungoverned space and become a threshold to attack our allies and neighbors, mostly immediately Tunisia and Algeria, but also there has been a very dramatic effect on Egypt as arms have flowed in from Libya into the Sinai and affected Israel's security. There is an issue of regional stability, particularly again with Egypt and Tunisia. The Libyan people deserve, after decades of a ruthless dictator, a better life in democracy and we certainly want to contribute to that.

And then there is the effect, I think, on our European allies with migration from Libya into Europe. But I would say the most urgent objective there is the counterterrorism objective.

Mr. DEUTCH. So just to continue that, Mr. Chollet, are we seeing fighters from Libya going to Syria for training and then returning to Libya and are there fighters from other North African countries going to Libya for training and then going back to their countries?

Mr. CHOLLET. Congressman, I think clearly Libya has become a magnet and it has been for many years and several years now a magnet for extremists, terrorists to go there. It is a vacant lot in many places in Libya and that tends to attract those types of people.

In terms of the flow both in and out, I would like to actually get back to you on that, maybe even provide you a classified answer if I could, because clearly it is something that is concerning and I know as Ambassador Patterson mentioned with our European allies and in particular, the Italians who are seeing a tremendous migration flow coming up out of Libya. Some of them are Libyans, but some of them are from other African countries that are using Libya as a transit point. The Italians are very worried that among those migrants will be extremists. So far, we have not seen that, but that is something we have got to be watching carefully just given the sheer volume of people flowing up north through the Mediterranean from Libya.

Mr. DEUTCH. Assistant Secretary Patterson, getting back to the know how that we can provide, what civil society programs are ongoing where we are taking the lead and where have we had positive impact? What else can we be doing to impact civil society in a positive way?

Ambassador PATTERSON. I think we have had a positive effect on the election process. I think we have had a positive effect on NDI training the parliamentarians and we plan to do more of that. IRI, for instance, is working with the Ministry of local government to work on local councils on decentralization. We have given a number of grants to civil society for small municipalities to encourage dialogue, to train, for instance, city councils and efforts like how to undertake a budget.

We are going to send up a number of—we have had women empowerment programs which have been quite successful, although very limited. And these are precisely the sorts of things that have had a limited impact, but we very much would like to expand. And they are not wildly expensive either. You can get a lot of bang for your buck here.

Mr. DEUTCH. Can you just go back and connect the dots then between these types of civil society programs and the reasons that it is important for us to be in Libya? How do these programs help address the rationale that we have to be in Libya to begin with?

Ambassador PATTERSON. Because, sir, there is essentially, no—let me put it this way, there are extremely limited government structures. And I think we were all taken by surprise when Gaddafi left, about the sheer lack of government institutions. So when civil society is mobilized and for instance when we empower these local councils and work with these local councils, they can make local government more responsive and learn how to engage with local government.

I think on the training, for instance, the parliamentarians or the political parties, this is entirely virgin territory. If we can train a political party, train people how to participate, it will help build Libyan institutions and we need to do it very broadly and aggressively.

Mr. DEUTCH. And finally, when you say it is a good return, good bang for the buck, can you give some numbers to that? How much do those sorts of programs cost?

Ambassador PATTERSON. Well, we have given grants, for instance, through NEFE and through USAID. We have given small grants, $15,000, $20,000, and some larger investments in the electoral process. But you can do a lot. Women's empowerment, for instance, all over the region, we have given very small grants, $25,000, $50,000 to NGOs to train women to start their own businesses and that is, I think, a very productive use of our funds.

Mr. DEUTCH. Very helpful. Thank you, both.

Ms. ROS-LEHTINEN. Thank you very much, Mr. Deutch. And we will turn to Mr. Weber of Texas.

Mr. WEBER. Thank you, Madam Chair. Secretary Patterson, in August 2011, Secretary Clinton—well, before I go there, let me do this. Recent unrest in Egypt. Of course, you saw the regime go down. You saw the military get involved. You saw Morsi go and

Sisi come up. Has that impacted Libya in any way? Do we see any kind of influx from Egypt since it borders Libya?

Ambassador PATTERSON. The Egyptians are very concerned about their border with Libya. It is about 700 miles essentially of sand. They have upped their presence on the border. They have a UAV base now on the border, so yes, they are quite concerned about that. I think there has been some success in stopping the weapons flow, but there were plenty of weapons that flowed into Egypt before they were active on the border.

Mr. WEBER. How many UAVs do they have—would you hazard a guess?

Ambassador PATTERSON. I don't know, but I can get that figure. They are quite new and they were supplied by a neighboring country. They are quite new.

Mr. WEBER. And who manufactured those UAVs?

Ambassador PATTERSON. I think they are a Chinese manufacturer, but supported by the United Arab Emirates. They were basically a military-assistance program from the United Arab Emirates.

Mr. WEBER. Okay, do we have good intel on the ground in Libya?

Ambassador PATTERSON. We have better and better intel on the ground, like most of these situations. And I can talk to you about that later. But let me be clear, there are huge portions of space in Libya that we do not have good information about, but our intelligence picture as is usually the case in these situations, the more you look, the more you learn. And I think our intelligence picture has gotten substantially better over time.

Mr. WEBER. How would you describe the relationship between the current Egyptian regime, if you will, and the Libyan regime?

Ambassador PATTERSON. I think it is professional and cordial, but what the Egyptians are extremely concerned about is the fighting in eastern Libya spilling over into their territory. So that is a major strategic concern for the Egyptians, but they have relations with the government. They have a large number of guest workers in Libya, always have had, and that is an important source of remittances.

Mr. WEBER. And are they maintaining forces along that 700-mile stretch?

Ambassador PATTERSON. They have maintained some forces there, but it is very hard to patrol, 700 miles of sand, of a border that is essentially unprotected.

Mr. WEBER. I am kind of going to back into my original question. In 2011, Secretary Clinton stated that ''the Libyan people made this revolution and they will lead the way forward, but they deserve our help. From the beginning, the United States has played a central role in marshalling the international response to the crisis in Libya. The United States will stand with the Libyan people and our international partners in the weeks and months ahead to help the Libyans write the next chapter in their history.''

Disappointingly, the decision to ''stand with our international partners'' seems to have been interpreted as allowing them, that is the Libyan people, to fail. Does the administration, in your view, bear any responsibility for the unfulfilled commitments, i.e., of our allies, NATO, U.N., European Union, EU? And what does ''allowing others to lead'' mean if the United States is not going to hold the others accountable for their commitments? Are we setting a dangerous precedent here?

Ambassador PATTERSON. Mr. Weber, I think all our international partners have found this situation extraordinarily difficult. And we have had a very high degree of cooperation, particularly with our European allies and also with the U.N. But let me give you a specific example on police training. I think it is widely recognized that the Libyans are desperate for professional police force because basically the militia performed that function. But our international partners have tried to do that. And what they have run into is tribal and ethnic conflict. They have run into difficult issues of vetting because they don't want to take people in their territory who are problematic. So I think it has been a challenge for everybody concerned to move forward in Libya.

Mr. WEBER. Okay. Thank you, Madam Chair. I yield back.

Ms. ROS-LEHTINEN. Thank you. Mr. Connolly is recognized.

Mr. CONNOLLY. Thank you, Madam Chairman. Ms. Patterson, is there a Libyan Government?

Ambassador PATTERSON. There is a prime minister. He is—yes, he is a transitional prime minister. There is a Parliament that will dissolve itself when the new Parliament comes into office. There is a constitutional drafting committee that seems like a relative bright spot. They have principles. They are meeting in committee. They are formulating the principles of the new Constitution. So there is some semblance of a government, yes.

Mr. CONNOLLY. Well, I mean the fact that people have titles doesn't form a government. I mean wasn't the Parliament just sort of temporarily abducted recently?

Ambassador PATTERSON. And the prime minister, too.

Mr. CONNOLLY. And the prime minister.

Ambassador PATTERSON. Yes, the last prime minister.

Mr. CONNOLLY. So they don't have a functioning police force. There is not really a functioning army.

Ambassador PATTERSON. No, their militia basically provide that function.

Mr. CONNOLLY. And there are lots of different militias?

Ambassador PATTERSON. Yes.

Mr. CONNOLLY. Some of which are friendly and some might be less friendly?

Ambassador PATTERSON. Some are friendly, some are less friendly, all are outside essentially the rule of law. I think our intelligence community counted something like 125 separate militia. But the leadership, what is surprising, Mr. Connolly, is not just leadership, there was nothing in the bureaucracy.

Mr. CONNOLLY. Yes.

Ambassador PATTERSON. So any time you wanted a contract signed and some of our businesses have really dramatic stories about this. You wanted a contract signed. You wanted a dispute resolved. You wanted to do what any government would consider normal business. It was almost impossible and that is what our corporations have run into, but they say with endurance, you can probably get this done. But there is nothing below this.

Mr. CONNOLLY. I am very sympathetic with that which is why I was maybe not as enthusiastic about the original revolution, not because I like Gaddafi, or that regime, but the question always is okay, what happens after?

Now what you just described is it is hard for me to see much of a difference between the Libya you are describing today and the Libya I visited 2 years ago. I mean it sounds like nothing has changed. When I landed in Tripoli, a militia guarded the airport. They were the security at the airport. We were talking about civil engagement and we were very excited about empowering women and other groups in society. And we were hopeful about elections that were pending. We were hoping a functional government might emerge from that. And I am not trying to lay blame, but it just sounds to me like not much has happened in Libya in 2 years. We are still talking the same language about the same hopes and not much has materialized other than maybe a deterioration in the internal security situation. Would that be a fair statement?

Ambassador PATTERSON. I think it would certainly be a fair statement that there has been a deterioration in the political situation and in the security situation, but Mr. Connolly, I don't see any real alternative to U.S. policy except to push ahead on these objectives. We have to stay there. We have to try and engage with the political actors who want to participate in political life and we have to try and improve the security situation.

Again, I think our overriding security and national interest simply demand that we try.

Mr. CONNOLLY. I agree with you, Ms. Patterson. But I guess what I am asking is what are reasonable milestones for measuring progress though? If, in fact, in the 2 years since I have been there we have seen deterioration rather than progress and that happens. Well, we don't want to be having this hearing 10 years hence saying well, yes, nothing has changed. The militias are still running it and there isn't a functional government and there is no army. And civil society, we are still trying to push for it, but not much has happened. I mean at what point do we say well, no, here are some real milestones we have to help them reach or they have to reach and that is the organizing principle for us and our allies in terms of aid investments and training programs and the like.

Ambassador PATTERSON. I think one of our first milestones would be formation of the General Purpose Force to have some true national security apparatus that could protect the population that was truly national in scope. And that strikes me as our most urgent priority and guideline as you would say that we have to do.

Mr. CONNOLLY. Mr. Chollet, would you mind commenting and then my time is up.

Mr. CHOLLET. Yes, sir. I would agree with Ambassador Patterson in terms of that initial milestone. I would say two of the things that have changed is what I mentioned previously which is the chemical weapons that have been undeclared were secured and many of the MANPADS, thousands of the MANPADS, were identified and destroyed. Those were two of the most urgent issues we faced——

Mr. CONNOLLY. I am sorry, I didn't hear the second one.

Mr. CHOLLET. The MANPADS, the shoulder fired air defense missiles. Thousands of those were identified and destroyed thanks to your support through funding to the State Department and to the Defense Department we were able to get that done. Now I don't want to sugarcoat it. We still have huge concerns about Libya's security, but some of these training efforts that are underway, moving too slow, we are frustrated by the bureaucratic dysfunction within Libya. If we can get that underway a year from now, hopefully we will be able to report on progress.

Mr. CONNOLLY. And one observation, I do think what has unfolded since the revolution in my opinion actually justifies the reluctance of the Obama administration to get too far into Libya despite importunities to the contrary because it was not at all clear what would succeed and Gaddafi, and what our leverage was. I mean sometimes we listen to rhetoric up here or in the press and even around the world and you would think somehow America is all powerful and just with the whisk of a wand we can make everything better and we can dictate the terms of how it gets better. That is not the case. And Libya is a great example of that.

Thank you, Madam Chairman.

Ms. ROS-LEHTINEN. Thank you, Mr. Connolly. Mr. DeSantis.

Mr. DESANTIS. Thank you, Madam Chairwoman. Secretary Patterson, back in 2009, Gaddafi was considered by both the Bush administration, the Obama administration, a lot of senior Republicans, I know in the Senate as being a key counterterrorism outlier. And I know there was a lot that happened in the intervening periods, but as we look at Libya today compared to that 2009 period where there seemed to be a lot of agreement in Washington from what I can tell, do Islamist Jihadists have a wider berth to operate in Libya today than they did 5 years ago?

Ambassador PATTERSON. Sure. If I might add, these societies run by ruthless dictators were never viable. They were always going to come crashing down. So we will just have to deal with that and there is no going back. But yes, they have now a terrorist safe haven in parts of eastern Libya.

Mr. DESANTIS. And there has been discussion about weaponry going to Syria and some of these other places. Is it the case that over the last 5 years Islamic Jihadists have had a greater access to weapons within Libya?

Ambassador PATTERSON. Everyone has had greater access to Libyan weapons. I think Gaddafi must have had enormous caches that were underestimated, but a lot of it has leaked onto the black and gray market as well.

Mr. DESANTIS. So it just seems to me—and then Ansar al-Sharia, the group responsible for the Benghazi attack in 2012, were they allied with Gaddafi or were they part of the "rebels" from 2011 as far as you can tell?

Ambassador PATTERSON. I don't know the answer to that, Congressman. I will have to get back to you.

Mr. DESANTIS. I know we picked up Abu Khattala. The administration had—I think it was under—we were under the impression in Congress that the administration's position about responding to the Benghazi attack was that they did not have the legal authority to conduct a kinetic attack against Ansar al-Sharia. Is that correct?

Is that the administration's position in terms of how they see their authority if they wanted to engage kinetically as a reprisal for the Benghazi attack?

Ambassador PATTERSON. Congressman, I think we better refer that question to the Justice Department. I would feel more comfortable with that. This gets into some tricky legal issues that I am not fully competent to answer.

Mr. DESANTIS. And is Abu Khattala, is he currently under the cognizance of the Defense Department or the Justice Department right now?

Ambassador PATTERSON. Again, Congressman, we should refer that question to the Justice Department which is managing this case.

Mr. DESANTIS. Can you say, Mr. Chollet, if the Defense Department has control over him?

Mr. CHOLLET. Sir, he is en route back to the United States. He faces criminal charges on three counts and I will refer all questions on this really to the Justice Department.

Mr. DESANTIS. I just wanted to, since you are here, just shift gears a little bit. A lot of people are concerned about what is going on in Iraq and a lot of focus, justifiably so, is focused on ISIS and clearly they are a problem. But I have really been alarmed by reports of the Shiite militias who are now being activated. It seems like they are the leading ''defense'' for the Malaki regime. It seems like a lot of the Iraqi army has melted away and most alarmingly is the presence of the Quds Force commander in Baghdad.

When I was in Iraq, as U.S. forces were defeating al-Qaeda in western Iraq, you had the Quds Force and you had the Shiite terror groups. They were blowing up hundreds of U.S. service members in Baghdad and eastern Iraq. And it is very, very concerning. And so what can you tell me about the footprint of Quds Force in particular in terms of being activated to fight against ISIS in Iraq? Either one, whichever one wants to take it.

Mr. CHOLLET. Congressman, I had seen those reports as well about the Iranian infiltration within Iraq and particularly among the Shia militia. I think what I would like to do, sir, is if we could get back to you perhaps in a closed setting and we could give you a full brief of our understanding of what is going on, particularly regarding the Shia issue. I think you are right to identify it. But I think, if we could, that would be the way I would like to handle that.

Ambassador PATTERSON. Congressman, yes, we have had a number of briefings up here with your colleagues, and we would be happy to come up here in the next few days and talk to you in a closed setting.

Mr. DESANTIS. Great. And I think that it seems to me when we debated Syria we kind of focused on Assad and he is backed by Hezbollah in Iran, and rightfully so. And there was not as much focus on the people. And I think most of them were more Islamist, in nature, fighting. But now that ISIS is moving in Iraq there is a lot of focus and again, understandably so. But I kind of feel like a lot of people are neglecting the extent to which the Shiite groups are anti-American. And, of course, Iran Quds Force and Prime Minister Netanyahu made a point this weekend, we want both of those groups on both sides to be weak ultimately. We don't want to choose one side or another and strengthen any of them unwittingly. So I really appreciate that. I look forward to hearing more and I yield back to the chair.

Ms. Ros-Lehtinen. Thank you very much, Mr. DeSantis. Dr. Yoho.

Mr. Yoho. Thank you, Madam Chair. Thank you for being here today, both of you. What is the status of the efforts to draft Libya's new Constitution?

Ambassador Patterson. Sir, the Constitution drafting committee, it has about 60 members. Some didn't take their seats. It is meeting in a little town called Bayda which is relatively peaceful. They have developed a set of principles. They have broken down into committees to discuss, to specialize and then they will go back and draft their Constitution. We don't know the timeframe, but so far so good. And we have been providing some assistance to civil society to engage with these drafters.

Mr. Yoho. Is there are a lot of Libyan civilian participation in that or is it the government figures or military figures? In the process of addressing the question such as civilian control of the military and the role of Islamic law, how does that equate in that?

Ambassador Patterson. Yes, those are all in the principles and have been discussed in the first stages. The constitutional drafters, members were elected. And one thing we have been trying to encourage, as have other international partners, is that these drafters engage with the public, with civil society as they draft the Constitution. I will send you a copy of the principles they are working off of.

Mr. Yoho. Do you know if they have property rights involved in that or is that going to be a component of that?

Ambassador Patterson. I have seen things on the oil revenues and frankly, I can't remember if they have property rights. But I will get back to you.

Mr. Yoho. Okay, let me switch gears. I would like to talk about the MANPADS. The report that I have got and I have read, the numbers are skewed. The numbers go all over the place. I have seen from 15,000 to over 30,000 MANPADS. A lot of them came from the United States of America, the way I understand it. And Mr. Chollet, you were talking about how we have spent $40 million tracking these down and trying to get rid of them. How is that money spent? Is that accounted for? I mean go through the process. Are we hiring contractors to do that? Is it our military? Who is actually doing the collection of those in the accountability of that?

Mr. Chollet. Yes, sir, absolutely. I can start. And first, I should say in terms of the number of MANPADS and again, this was the most urgent issue, one of the most urgent issues we faced several years ago right after Gaddafi's fall, the estimates widely varied, in part, because we just didn't know. Gaddafi was not the world's best bookkeeper in terms of what he actually had in stock and also the estimates, the high end which we operated from was an estimate driven from our assessment of the amount of MANPADS they had acquired since the '70s. So that did not account for the MANPADS they used, the MANPADS that had been stolen, the MANPADS that were broken over the past 30-plus years. So nevertheless, it was a State Department administered program. It was done by contractors, primarily, but there was a team, a team at the State Ambassador, I will let Ambassador Patterson speak to this more, that specializes in MANPADS that work out of the Political-Military Affairs Bureau at the Department of State. And they went into Libya soon after the fall of Gaddafi and began a program first to identify the stockpile, assess what they had and then begin the process of destroying those MANPADS.

Mr. YOHO. Okay, my concern is, you know, I look back at when President Obama demanded that Gaddafi must step down. I remember that so succinctly and I see that same thing going now in Iraq. Karzai must step down. And for us not to know what is on the ground, what is there and what the replacement is going to be to fill that vacuum just scares us to death and I know it scares a lot of our partners in the Middle East to death. And I don't want to make the same mistakes we made in Libya. You must step down and they say be careful what you wish for, because if it did happen, we weren't in a position I don't feel that we could get somebody in there immediately that we could work with. Correct me if I am wrong on that.

Mr. CHOLLET. See, Iraq and Libya are completely different cases. I would argue we probably have a better intel picture right now of what is going on in Iraq than we did in Libya under Gaddafi, that is for sure. And all I can say, sir, again not to in any way minimize the challenge we are facing in Libya today, we have shown through some of these relatively modest programs that we have been able to take care of what we consider to be urgent security threats we faced in terms of the chemical weapons and the MANPADS.

Mr. YOHO. Madam Chair, I yield back. Thank you.

Ms. ROS-LEHTINEN. Thank you so much. I thank the panelists for being with us. We enjoy that you are always accessible and we remain committed to working with you to see if we can fix this mess. Thank you so much and with that the subcommittee is adjourned.

[Whereupon, at 3:10 p.m., the subcommittee was adjourned.]

A P P E N D I X

Material Submitted for the Record

SUBCOMMITTEE HEARING NOTICE
COMMITTEE ON FOREIGN AFFAIRS
U.S. HOUSE OF REPRESENTATIVES
WASHINGTON, DC 20515-6128

Subcommittee on the Middle East and North Africa
Chairman Ileana Ros-Lehtinen (R-FL), Chairman

June 18, 2014

TO: MEMBERS OF THE COMMITTEE ON FOREIGN AFFAIRS

You are respectfully requested to attend an OPEN hearing of the Committee on Foreign Affairs, to be held by the Subcommittee on the Middle East and North Africa in Room 2172 of the Rayburn House Office Building (and available live on the Committee website at http://www.ForeignAffairs.house.gov):

DATE: Wednesday, June 25, 2014

TIME: 2:00 p.m.

SUBJECT: Libya at a Crossroads: A Faltering Transition

WITNESSES: The Honorable Anne W. Patterson
                   Assistant Secretary
                   Bureau of Near Eastern Affairs
                   U.S. Department of State

                   The Honorable Derek Chollet
                   Assistant Secretary of Defense for International Security Affairs
                   U.S. Department of Defense

By Direction of the Chairman

COMMITTEE ON FOREIGN AFFAIRS

MINUTES OF SUBCOMMITTEE ON _____ *the Middle East and North Africa* _____ HEARING

Day___ *Wednesday*___Date_____ *6/25/14* _____Room_____ *2172* _____

Starting Time ___ *2:03 p.m.* ___Ending Time ___ *3:10 p.m.* ___

Recesses | *0* | (____to ____) (____to ____) (____to ____) (____to ____) (____to ____) (____to ____)

Presiding Member(s)

Chairman Ros-Lehtinen

Check all of the following that apply:

Open Session ☑   Electronically Recorded (taped) ☑
Executive (closed) Session ☐   Stenographic Record ☑
Televised ☑

TITLE OF HEARING:

Libya at a Crossroads: A Faltering Transition

SUBCOMMITTEE MEMBERS PRESENT:

Chairman Ros-Lehtinen, Ranking Member Deutch, Reps. Weber, Chabot, DeSantis, Yoho, Cotton, Kennedy, and Cicilline.

NON-SUBCOMMITTEE MEMBERS PRESENT: *(Mark with an * if they are not members of full committee.)*

Reps. Royce and Rohrabacher

HEARING WITNESSES: Same as meeting notice attached? Yes ☑ No ☐
(If "no", please list below and include title, agency, department, or organization.)

STATEMENTS FOR THE RECORD: *(List any statements submitted for the record.)*

SFR - Rep. Royce
SFR - Rep. Connolly

TIME SCHEDULED TO RECONVENE _____
or
TIME ADJOURNED___ *3:10 p.m.* ___

Subcommittee Staff Director

42

Statement by
A Omar Turbi
Expert - U.S Libya Relations
Before the Committee on International Relations
U.S. House of Representatives
Libya at a Crossroads: A Faltering Transition
Wednesday, June 25th, 2014

I am honored to have the opportunity to provide testimony to your distinguished committee on the subject- **Libya at a Crossroads: A Faltering Transition.**

I wish to express my sincere appreciation for the continued support by the United States of the Libyan people. If it were not for the bold push by the United States to force Libyan dictator Muamar Qaddafi from power in 2011, Libya and the Libyan people would not have been liberated.

It has become abundantly clear, three years after the fall of the Qaddafi regime; the Libyan people have not been able to establish viable democratic institutions, and a functioning state. The crisis at present has reached alarming levels and threatens the peace and security, not only of Libya but also of North Africa, the Sahel countries and the Mediterranean. The prospects of an intractable crisis are looming, and Libya is on the brink of becoming a failed state at the center of a critical region of the World.

Many current and former senior Libyan government officials recognize the requirement for international intervention.

Today the Libyan people are electing a new 200 member legislative body to replace the outgoing General National Congress (GNC) of which term had expired in February this year. Although many Libyans are optimistic at the prospects of a new beginning, I am pessimistic due to anticipated low voter turn out due to lack of public security, poor planning and the possibility of more of the same of less qualified new members of a new GNC.

The Libyan people are grateful for the on going engagement by the United States to help contain further crisis. Myself, and a group of prominent Libyan experts submitted an initiative to Secretary General of the United Nations Ban Ki Moon on June 5th, 2014, some of its content is provided below. Although we are pleased that the UN has recently undertaken steps along the lines of our proposed initiative, more effort by the U.S as a powerful member of the Security Council is needed for effective UN intervention.

The mission of such intervention, however, must be under the UN and in accordance to UN resolutions adopted in 2011 under chapter 7. **It must be noted that during the course of drafting and planning the subject initiative we spoke with many Libyan government officials, current and former holders of senior positions, former prime ministers, and deputy prime ministers, members of the General National Congress (GNC) and Libyan Ambassadors abroad. The vast majority who reviewed the draft and final version of the initiative have applauded its content and endorsed the call for IMMEDIATE AND ACTIVE INTERNATIONAL INTERVENTION IN THE ONGOING LIBYA CRISIS and pledged their support. While we wanted to publish their names, they, however, requested their names to be withheld due to personal and security reasons.** A summary of the initiative is provided below from (1) through (5):

1- Strengthen and expand the mandate of the United Nations Support Mission in Libya (UNSMIL), under the existing UN resolutions adopted in 2011, to actively convene a conference of all Libyan armed militias and all key political groups. In such conference the UN would start and directly administer a credible and serious process of national reconciliation, disarmament, and amnesty programs between all parties in order to go beyond all grievances of the past including those before February 17, 2011. The UN should act, as the neutral party Libya needs now the most and take the lead in managing and guaranteeing the enforcement of any outcome by all means referenced in the current active resolutions with the support of the International Community.

2- UN should guide a new political road map and democratic mechanisms for the establishment of a legislative body as soon as possible that can replace the current General National Congress (GNC) and provide direct support and effective guidelines for the nominations, elections and congressional conduct for the new GNC.

3- The UN should provide more direct and active support for the new constitution's drafting and ratification process, already in place by the recently elected committee in charge of drafting the constitution, as well as greater support for the adoption of the new constitution in a national referendum to be managed by the UN.

4- Work closely with the national army of Libya, under the authority of a newly elected legislative body and its nominated government to stabilize the country and create viable and secure Libyan territories for all its civilian population whom may potentially be caught within the warring factions in different regions of the country.

5- Support the inclusion of all Libyans regardless of beliefs or political opinion in the process of a peaceful political transition including all political exiles and war refugees of over 1.5 million Libyans scattered between Egypt and Tunisia.

Honorable Congresswomen and Honorable Congressmen, I believe in order for our foreign policy to succeed with Libya and the region, we must pursue one that is truly based on enlightened self-interest. I would like to make the following recommendations:

(a). Islamists in the region have become a reality of the political landscape. Therefore, we must not view and lump extremist Islamists with none extremists ones. The dynamics of political Islam in Libya are different than those in Egypt. The failure of the Muslim Brotherhood in Egypt may not reflect the realities of the Muslim Brotherhood in Libya. I am a strong advocate of carrying out a constructive and direct dialogue with the leadership of the Muslim Brotherhood of Libya. I have had discussions with their leadership. I believe they have genuine interest in a more successful democracy in Libya because of lessons learned from the Egyptian experience.

(b). Support for democratic processes in Libya and assistance in the construction of Libyan institutions has to go beyond encouraging the work of American NGO's. Libya's diplomatic and economic missions around the world are dysfunctional and require overhaul and rebuilding from the ground up. We must not be restricted by sovereignty matters. The U.S government should offer to help the anticipated emerging new Libyan government to build a more effective Libyan diplomatic corp around the world.

 (c). We must work closer with our European allies to stem the growing flow of migrants from the African sub Sahara through Libya. We have not done enough to assist the interim Libyan governments install working systems for control of Libyan borders.

(d). I encourage current programs underway by the U.S in training Libyan military personnel in Libya's quest to build a national army. We should learn from any set backs and continue with greater numbers and speed.

(e). We must learn lessons from the attack on the U.S Consulate in Benghazi in September, 2012. I believe the U.S clandestine operations in and around Benghazi in trying to identify Al-Qaeda elements leading up to that time of the attack on the Consulate may have contributed to the assault on the U.S Consulate and the death of U.S Ambassador Chris Stevens and four U.S servicemen.

Honorable Congresswomen and Honorable Congressmen Libya's unique and beautiful coast line, year long lush green mountains, beautiful desert and its close proximity to Europe and the gates of Africa, its treasures of thousands of years of history, and most of all its wealth with natural resources place Libya as an important player on the world scene. Thank you.